also by misty copeland

Firebird (illustrated by Christopher Myers)
Life in Motion (Atria 2014)
Life in Motion: Young Readers Edition
Ballerina Body

your life
in motion

your life in motion

A guided journal for discovering the fire in you

MISTY COPELAND

Aladdin
NEW YORK LONDON TORONTO SYDNEY NEW DELHI

ALADDIN

An imprint of Simon & Schuster Children's Publishing Division

1230 Avenue of the Americas, New York, New York 10020

First Aladdin hardcover edition November 2018

Text copyright © 2018 by Misty Copeland

Cover photograph copyright © 2018 by Ken Browar and Deborah Ory

Photo courtesy of American Ballet Theatre

For information about special discounts for bulk purchases, please contact Simon & Schuster

Special Sales at 1-866-506-1949 or business@simonandschuster.com.

The Simon & Schuster Speakers Bureau can bring authors to your live event.

For more information or to book an event contact the Simon & Schuster Speakers Bureau

at 1-866-248-3049 or visit our website at www.simonspeakers.com.

Cover designed by Dan Potash

Interior designed by Mike Rosamilia

The text of this book was set in Adobe Garamond Pro.

Manufactured in the United States of America 1018 RR2

2 4 6 8 10 9 7 5 3 1

Library of Congress Control Number 2018953283

ISBN 978-1-5344-4302-0 (hc)

introduction

When I was younger, I was incredibly shy. It was hard for me to express myself publicly, so writing in my journal was a wonderful way for me to process big moments in my life. It was an outlet, a safe space where I could share my feelings.

These journals eventually became the foundation for my memoir, *Life in Motion*. Looking back through everything, I realized that the beauty of writing is that you will always have an official "record" of snapshots of your life. I wrote about the time I was told I would officially apprentice with the main company of the American Ballet Theatre. I detailed the feelings I had after performing in *La Bayadère*, under difficult circumstances, as well as after my breakout role in *Firebird*. I also turned to my journal after receiving the devastating news that I would have to sit out a season, thanks to several stress fractures that needed surgery and time to heal.

The magical thing about these journals isn't just having a reminder of the moments themselves—it's being able to look back and truly have the ability to pinpoint exactly how you were feeling at a specific time.

While many things have changed in my life, it has been so interesting to look back and see where my journey has taken me, to see how I have grown from each experience, good and bad.

Putting pen to paper and just writing it out has been a source of great comfort to me, and I hope this journal will become a safe space for you—a space to map out your secrets and fears, your goals and dreams, and everything in between.

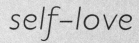
self-love

How would you describe yourself?

_____

_____

_____

_____

_____

_____

_____

_____

_____

_____

_____

_____

_____

_____

_____

_____

_____

_____

_____

_____

_____

_____

How does your BFF see you?

_____

_____

_____

_____

_____

_____

_____

_____

_____

_____

_____

_____

_____

_____

_____

_____

_____

_____

_____

_____

_____

_____

_____

_____

If you could make an inspiration board of your life currently, what would it look like? Paste images below!

Early in my career I faced all kinds of criticism about my body—from the color of my skin to my physical shape and weight. I had a tricky relationship with food and struggled with my self-image. And I still face those critics! But over time, I've learned to love my body and appreciate the strength that my body has had since I was young, before I even stepped foot in a dance studio. And not just physical strength, but the inner strength I have gained through my experiences both in and out of the dance world.

What are three things you love about you? Why?

1. _____

_____

_____

_____

2. _____

_____

_____

_____

_____

3. _____

_____

_____

_____

I am very aware and proud of the expectations that people have of me, both as a dancer and as a role model. And it's a privilege to be in that position. But like anyone else, I am not immune to having a bad day! When I was performing *Swan Lake* recently, someone criticized me online for not doing the full thirty-two fouettés in the famous turn sequence during one performance. As I said then, ballerinas are not defined by the number of fouettés we do; rather, we are defined by how we, as artists, move people. I want people, especially kids, to know that it's okay to make mistakes, and to know that I am always learning and growing. I see learning moments in all experiences, good and bad.

What setbacks have you faced recently?

_____

_____

_____

_____

_____

_____

_____

_____

How did you react?

_____

_____

_____

_____

_____

_____

If you could do it over again,
what would you do differently?

_____

_____

_____

_____

_____

What would you do the same?

_____

_____

_____

_____

_____

_____

My schedule, especially during the American Ballet Theatre season, is jam-packed! It's important for me to balance this with time to just unwind and relax. I love spending time with my husband, family, and friends. One of my favorite ways to relax is to cook and create healthy recipes!

What are your favorite ways to relax? Why?

_____

_____

_____

_____

_____

_____

_____

_____

_____

_____

_____

_____

_____

I often reach for nuts and fresh fruit before rehearsals to give me energy. I really love to eat healthfully, but I also like to enjoy things like pizza and ice cream! It's all about balance.

What are some of your favorite foods?

I normally spend around seven to eight hours in the ballet studio at least five days a week, and more when I'm prepping for the ballet season. Sundays I rest, and Mondays are my "days off," which I usually use to work on my partnerships and charity work. What is a typical week like for you?

MONDAY

_____
_____
_____
_____

TUESDAY

_____
_____
_____
_____

WEDNESDAY

_____
_____
_____
_____

THURSDAY

_____
_____
_____
_____

FRIDAY

_____
_____
_____
_____

SATURDAY

_____
_____
_____
_____

SUNDAY

_____
_____
_____
_____

In 2018 I launched my very own line of lifestyle and athletic clothing from Under Armour! It was an incredible experience, and it was a joy to use my creativity in a different way. I want to feel good and look good in the clothes I wear, so that is how I approached designing this line.

What outfit do you feel most confident in?

_____

_____

_____

_____

_____

_____

_____

_____

_____

_____

_____

_____

_____

_____

What is your favorite look for school?
Describe or draw it below!

_____

_____

_____

_____

_____

_____

_____

_____

_____

_____

_____

_____

_____

_____

_____

_____

_____

_____

_____

_____

_____

_____

_____

_____

When I first moved to New York City, it was an exciting time for me. I've worked very hard to achieve what I have professionally, but I also give a lot of credit to some incredible mentors I've had along the way.

Raven Wilkinson was the first black American to dance with a major ballet touring troupe. She had to face the risk of arrest, and even death, to tour in the South during the 1950s. She was a trailblazer, and Raven has become both a mentor and a friend.

During my first few years at the American Ballet Theatre, I met and performed with the legendary Prince. He pushed me artistically and gave me a creative freedom that I really appreciated during our collaboration.

Who do you admire?

_____

_____

_____

_____

_____

_____

How have they influenced you?

_____

_____

_____

_____

_____

_____

_____

_____

_____

_____

_____

_____

_____

_____

_____

_____

_____

_____

_____

_____

_____

A lot of my time is spent in the dance studio or onstage. And outside the studio I'm often going to meetings for my other ventures and charity work. I like to be prepared for anything! I always have dance shoes—ballet slippers and my pointe shoes—leg warmers, my phone, snacks, and some toiletries in my bag, so I'm always prepared!

What's inside your bag? What item do you reach for the most?

_____

_____

_____

_____

What is your favorite item?

_____

_____

Why?

_____

_____

_____

_____

One of the best parts of my job is connecting with fans—especially YOU! I am lucky to receive beautiful letters from people all over the globe who are kind enough to share their stories with me.

Write a letter to your future self a year from now.

_____

_____

_____

_____

_____

_____

_____

_____

_____

_____

_____

_____

_____

_____

_____

_____

_____

Write a letter to your eighteen-year-old self.

We all have gifts that we can use to inspire and nurture others. I hope that I am able to inspire the next generation of dancers, and I try to use my platform to advocate for diversity within the ballet community.

What are three ways you feel you inspire others?

1. _____

_____

_____

_____

_____

2. _____

_____

_____

_____

_____

3. _____

_____

_____

_____

_____

It is important to surround yourself with support—whether the support comes from your parents, other family members, trusted adults, good friends, or mentors in your community. There are days when it might be hard to trust yourself or trust that what you are doing is the right path, and your trusted circle can support and guide you.

Who would you consider to be your trusted circle of support? In what ways do they each support you?

_____

_____

_____

_____

_____

_____

_____

_____

_____

_____

_____

_____

_____

_____

Jumping into the unknown is always a little scary. When I first started ballet at my local Boys & Girls Club in San Pedro, California, I had to be encouraged by my drill team instructor and ballet teacher for quite a while before I put my hand on the barre for the first time. Obviously it was the best thing I ever did!

What are some things that scare you? Why?

_____

_____

_____

_____

_____

_____

_____

_____

_____

_____

_____

_____

_____

_____

Name some things you have not done yet but would like to try.

Find something that brings back a great memory.
Tape it below!

school days

Growing up, I enjoyed school. I was even hall monitor and class treasurer during my middle-school years!

What are some clubs and activities that you want to do this school year?

_____

_____

_____

_____

_____

_____

_____

_____

What is one new thing you learned today at school?

_____

_____

_____

_____

_____

_____

_____

_____

Our successes are a credit to the people holding us up, and I wouldn't have gotten to where I am today without the guidance of many teachers along the way.

Who is your favorite teacher, and why?

_____

_____

_____

_____

_____

_____

_____

_____

_____

_____

_____

_____

_____

_____

_____

_____

_____

_____

What is your favorite class, and why?

_____

_____

_____

_____

_____

_____

_____

_____

_____

_____

_____

_____

_____

_____

_____

_____

_____

_____

_____

_____

_____

Some things come naturally, and some come with more struggles.

Which class do you have the most trouble with?

_____

_____

Why do you think that is?

_____

_____

_____

_____

_____

_____

_____

_____

_____

_____

_____

_____

_____

_____

I didn't start dancing until I was thirteen, which is considered late in the ballet world! Because I started so late, I had to focus and work that much harder to make up for lost time.

What do you think are some steps you can take to make your hardest class easier for you?

_____

_____

_____

_____

_____

_____

_____

_____

_____

_____

_____

_____

_____

_____

_____

_____

Describe the best school day you've ever had.

_____

_____

_____

_____

_____

_____

_____

_____

_____

_____

_____

_____

_____

_____

_____

_____

_____

_____

_____

What was the best field trip you've ever been on? What happened?

_____

_____

_____

_____

_____

_____

_____

_____

_____

_____

_____

_____

_____

_____

_____

_____

_____

_____

_____

_____

_____

Paste pictures of your field trip here!

My biggest goal was to become a principal dancer for the American Ballet Theatre. Through a lot of hard work and sacrifice, I was able to achieve that in 2015. But just because I have reached that goal doesn't mean I'm done! I am always setting goals for myself that keep me focused and motivated.

What are your goals for the year?

_____

_____

_____

What are your goals for the next five years?

_____

_____

_____

What are your goals for the next ten years?

_____

_____

_____

_____

_____

Identifying your goals is just the first step! Sometimes it helps to write down a plan of action.

What is your academic goal for the school year?

_____

_____

_____

_____

_____

_____

_____

How are you going to achieve this?

_____

_____

_____

_____

_____

_____

_____

_____

_____

School is more than just the classes, of course. I always try to choose kindness and make sure my friends know I appreciate them.

List some of your social goals for this school year.

_____

_____

_____

_____

_____

_____

_____

_____

_____

_____

_____

_____

_____

_____

_____

_____

_____

Create an inspiration board! Cut and paste images that inspire you to reach for your dreams.

memories

Your past can be a great source of inspiration for future goals. My own childhood has inspired my career in so many ways. The first memory I have is of performing at a local talent competition when I was five years old.

What is your earliest memory?

_____

_____

_____

_____

_____

_____

_____

_____

_____

_____

_____

_____

_____

_____

_____

_____

Create an inspiration board! Cut and paste images that remind you of your early childhood.

What are some of your happiest memories?

_____

_____

_____

_____

_____

_____

_____

_____

_____

_____

_____

_____

_____

_____

_____

_____

_____

_____

_____

_____

_____

_____

Just as there are happy memories, there are always going to be some more unpleasant memories. However, I always try to see the unhappier memories as learning experiences.

What was one learning experience for you, and what did you take away from it?

_____

_____

_____

_____

_____

_____

_____

_____

_____

_____

_____

_____

_____

_____

_____

_____

reflections

Sometimes it can be helpful—and fun!—to think back on your day. The next section is for you to help remind yourself about all the positive things and lessons you learned during your day.

Date:

_____

Word of the day:

_____

Today I am grateful for . . .

_____

_____

_____

_____

What is one good thing that happened today?

_____

_____

_____

_____

What is one lesson I learned today?

_____

_____

_____

Date:

Word of the day:

Today I am grateful for . . .

What is one good thing that happened today?

What is one lesson I learned today?

Date:

Word of the day:

Today I am grateful for . . .

What is one good thing that happened today?

What is one lesson I learned today?

Date:

_____

Word of the day:

_____

Today I am grateful for . . .

_____

_____

_____

_____

What is one good thing that happened today?

_____

_____

_____

_____

What is one lesson I learned today?

_____

_____

_____

Date:

Word of the day:

Today I am grateful for . . .

What is one good thing that happened today?

What is one lesson I learned today?

Date:

_____

Word of the day:

_____

Today I am grateful for . . .

_____

_____

_____

_____

What is one good thing that happened today?

_____

_____

_____

_____

What is one lesson I learned today?

_____

_____

_____

Date:

Word of the day:

Today I am grateful for . . .

What is one good thing that happened today?

What is one lesson I learned today?

Date:

_____

Word of the day:

_____

Today I am grateful for . . .

_____

_____

_____

_____

What is one good thing that happened today?

_____

_____

_____

_____

What is one lesson I learned today?

_____

_____

_____

Date:

_____

Word of the day:

_____

Today I am grateful for . . .

_____

_____

_____

_____

What is one good thing that happened today?

_____

_____

_____

_____

What is one lesson I learned today?

_____

_____

_____

Date:

_____

Word of the day:

_____

Today I am grateful for . . .

_____
_____
_____
_____

What is one good thing that happened today?

_____
_____
_____
_____

What is one lesson I learned today?

_____
_____
_____

Date:

_____

Word of the day:

_____

Today I am grateful for . . .

_____

_____

_____

_____

What is one good thing that happened today?

_____

_____

_____

_____

What is one lesson I learned today?

_____

_____

_____

Date:

_____

Word of the day:

_____

Today I am grateful for . . .

_____

_____

_____

_____

What is one good thing that happened today?

_____

_____

_____

_____

What is one lesson I learned today?

_____

_____

_____

Date:

_____

Word of the day:

_____

Today I am grateful for . . .

_____
_____
_____
_____

What is one good thing that happened today?

_____
_____
_____
_____

What is one lesson I learned today?

_____
_____
_____

Date:

_____

Word of the day:

_____

Today I am grateful for . . .

_____

_____

_____

_____

What is one good thing that happened today?

_____

_____

_____

_____

What is one lesson I learned today?

_____

_____

_____

Date:

Word of the day:

Today I am grateful for . . .

What is one good thing that happened today?

What is one lesson I learned today?

Date:

_____

Word of the day:

_____

Today I am grateful for . . .

_____
_____
_____
_____

What is one good thing that happened today?

_____
_____
_____
_____

What is one lesson I learned today?

_____
_____
_____
_____

Date:

Word of the day:

Today I am grateful for . . .

What is one good thing that happened today?

What is one lesson I learned today?

Date:

_____

Word of the day:

_____

Today I am grateful for . . .

_____

_____

_____

_____

What is one good thing that happened today?

_____

_____

_____

_____

What is one lesson I learned today?

_____

_____

_____

Date:

_____

Word of the day:

_____

Today I am grateful for . . .

_____

_____

_____

_____

What is one good thing that happened today?

_____

_____

_____

_____

What is one lesson I learned today?

_____

_____

_____

Date:

_____

Word of the day:

_____

Today I am grateful for . . .

_____
_____
_____
_____

What is one good thing that happened today?

_____
_____
_____
_____

What is one lesson I learned today?

_____
_____
_____

Date:

_____

Word of the day:

_____

Today I am grateful for . . .

_____

_____

_____

_____

What is one good thing that happened today?

_____

_____

_____

_____

What is one lesson I learned today?

_____

_____

_____

Date:

_____

Word of the day:

_____

Today I am grateful for . . .

_____

_____

_____

_____

What is one good thing that happened today?

_____

_____

_____

_____

What is one lesson I learned today?

_____

_____

_____

Date:

_____

Word of the day:

_____

Today I am grateful for . . .

_____
_____
_____
_____

What is one good thing that happened today?

_____
_____
_____
_____

What is one lesson I learned today?

_____
_____
_____

Date:

Word of the day:

Today I am grateful for . . .

What is one good thing that happened today?

What is one lesson I learned today?

Date:

_____

Word of the day:

_____

Today I am grateful for . . .

_____
_____
_____
_____

What is one good thing that happened today?

_____
_____
_____
_____

What is one lesson I learned today?

_____
_____
_____

Date:

_____

Word of the day:

_____

Today I am grateful for . . .

_____

_____

_____

_____

What is one good thing that happened today?

_____

_____

_____

_____

What is one lesson I learned today?

_____

_____

_____

Date:

_____

Word of the day:

_____

Today I am grateful for . . .

_____

_____

_____

_____

What is one good thing that happened today?

_____

_____

_____

_____

What is one lesson I learned today?

_____

_____

_____

_____

Date:

_____

Word of the day:

_____

Today I am grateful for . . .

_____
_____
_____
_____

What is one good thing that happened today?

_____
_____
_____
_____

What is one lesson I learned today?

_____
_____
_____

Date:

Word of the day:

Today I am grateful for . . .

What is one good thing that happened today?

What is one lesson I learned today?

Date:

_____

Word of the day:

_____

Today I am grateful for . . .

_____

_____

_____

_____

What is one good thing that happened today?

_____

_____

_____

_____

What is one lesson I learned today?

_____

_____

_____

Date:

_____

Word of the day:

_____

Today I am grateful for . . .

_____

_____

_____

_____

What is one good thing that happened today?

_____

_____

_____

_____

What is one lesson I learned today?

_____

_____

_____

Date:

_____

Word of the day:

_____

Today I am grateful for . . .

_____

_____

_____

_____

What is one good thing that happened today?

_____

_____

_____

_____

What is one lesson I learned today?

_____

_____

_____

Date:

_____

Word of the day:

_____

Today I am grateful for . . .

_____

_____

_____

_____

What is one good thing that happened today?

_____

_____

_____

_____

What is one lesson I learned today?

_____

_____

_____

Date:

_____

Word of the day:

_____

Today I am grateful for . . .

_____

_____

_____

_____

What is one good thing that happened today?

_____

_____

_____

_____

What is one lesson I learned today?

_____

_____

_____

Date:

_____

Word of the day:

_____

Today I am grateful for . . .

_____

_____

_____

_____

What is one good thing that happened today?

_____

_____

_____

_____

What is one lesson I learned today?

_____

_____

_____

Date:

_____

Word of the day:

_____

Today I am grateful for . . .

_____

_____

_____

_____

What is one good thing that happened today?

_____

_____

_____

_____

What is one lesson I learned today?

_____

_____

_____

Date:

_____

Word of the day:

_____

Today I am grateful for . . .

_____

_____

_____

_____

What is one good thing that happened today?

_____

_____

_____

_____

What is one lesson I learned today?

_____

_____

_____

Date:

_____

Word of the day:

_____

Today I am grateful for . . .

_____

_____

_____

_____

What is one good thing that happened today?

_____

_____

_____

_____

What is one lesson I learned today?

_____

_____

_____

Date:

Word of the day:

Today I am grateful for . . .

What is one good thing that happened today?

What is one lesson I learned today?

Date:

_____

Word of the day:

_____

Today I am grateful for . . .

_____

_____

_____

_____

What is one good thing that happened today?

_____

_____

_____

_____

What is one lesson I learned today?

_____

_____

_____

Date:

Word of the day:

Today I am grateful for . . .

What is one good thing that happened today?

What is one lesson I learned today?

Date:

_____

Word of the day:

_____

Today I am grateful for . . .

_____

_____

_____

_____

What is one good thing that happened today?

_____

_____

_____

_____

What is one lesson I learned today?

_____

_____

_____

Date:

_____

Word of the day:

_____

Today I am grateful for . . .

_____
_____
_____
_____

What is one good thing that happened today?

_____
_____
_____
_____

What is one lesson I learned today?

_____
_____
_____
_____

Date:

Word of the day:

Today I am grateful for . . .

What is one good thing that happened today?

What is one lesson I learned today?

Date:

_____

Word of the day:

_____

Today I am grateful for . . .

_____

_____

_____

_____

What is one good thing that happened today?

_____

_____

_____

_____

What is one lesson I learned today?

_____

_____

_____

Date:

_____

Word of the day:

_____

Today I am grateful for . . .

_____

_____

_____

_____

What is one good thing that happened today?

_____

_____

_____

_____

What is one lesson I learned today?

_____

_____

_____

Date:

_____

Word of the day:

_____

Today I am grateful for . . .

_____

_____

_____

_____

What is one good thing that happened today?

_____

_____

_____

_____

What is one lesson I learned today?

_____

_____

_____

Date:

_____

Word of the day:

_____

Today I am grateful for . . .

_____

_____

_____

_____

What is one good thing that happened today?

_____

_____

_____

_____

What is one lesson I learned today?

_____

_____

_____

Date:

Word of the day:

Today I am grateful for . . .

What is one good thing that happened today?

What is one lesson I learned today?

Date:

_____

Word of the day:

_____

Today I am grateful for . . .

_____
_____
_____
_____

What is one good thing that happened today?

_____
_____
_____
_____

What is one lesson I learned today?

_____
_____
_____

Date:

_____

Word of the day:

_____

Today I am grateful for . . .

_____
_____
_____
_____

What is one good thing that happened today?

_____
_____
_____
_____

What is one lesson I learned today?

_____
_____
_____

Date:

_____

Word of the day:

_____

Today I am grateful for . . .

_____

_____

_____

_____

What is one good thing that happened today?

_____

_____

_____

_____

What is one lesson I learned today?

_____

_____

_____

Date:

_____

Word of the day:

_____

Today I am grateful for . . .

_____

_____

_____

_____

What is one good thing that happened today?

_____

_____

_____

_____

What is one lesson I learned today?

_____

_____

_____

_____

Date:

_____

Word of the day:

_____

Today I am grateful for . . .

_____

_____

_____

_____

What is one good thing that happened today?

_____

_____

_____

_____

What is one lesson I learned today?

_____

_____

_____

_____

Date:

_____

Word of the day:

_____

Today I am grateful for . . .

_____

_____

_____

_____

What is one good thing that happened today?

_____

_____

_____

_____

What is one lesson I learned today?

_____

_____

_____

Date:

_____

Word of the day:

_____

Today I am grateful for . . .

_____

_____

_____

_____

What is one good thing that happened today?

_____

_____

_____

_____

What is one lesson I learned today?

_____

_____

_____

_____

Date:

Word of the day:

Today I am grateful for . . .

What is one good thing that happened today?

What is one lesson I learned today?

Date:

_____

Word of the day:

_____

Today I am grateful for . . .

_____

_____

_____

_____

What is one good thing that happened today?

_____

_____

_____

_____

What is one lesson I learned today?

_____

_____

_____

_____

Date:

Word of the day:

Today I am grateful for . . .

What is one good thing that happened today?

What is one lesson I learned today?

Date:

_____

Word of the day:

_____

Today I am grateful for . . .

_____

_____

_____

_____

What is one good thing that happened today?

_____

_____

_____

_____

What is one lesson I learned today?

_____

_____

_____

_____

Date:

_____

Word of the day:

_____

Today I am grateful for . . .

_____

_____

_____

_____

What is one good thing that happened today?

_____

_____

_____

_____

What is one lesson I learned today?

_____

_____

_____

Date:

Word of the day:

Today I am grateful for . . .

What is one good thing that happened today?

What is one lesson I learned today?

Date:

Word of the day:

Today I am grateful for . . .

What is one good thing that happened today?

What is one lesson I learned today?

Date:

_____

Word of the day:

_____

Today I am grateful for . . .

_____

_____

_____

_____

What is one good thing that happened today?

_____

_____

_____

_____

What is one lesson I learned today?

_____

_____

_____

_____

Date:

Word of the day:

Today I am grateful for . . .

What is one good thing that happened today?

What is one lesson I learned today?

Date:

_____

Word of the day:

_____

Today I am grateful for . . .

_____

_____

_____

_____

What is one good thing that happened today?

_____

_____

_____

_____

What is one lesson I learned today?

_____

_____

_____

Date:

_____

Word of the day:

_____

Today I am grateful for . . .

_____

_____

_____

_____

What is one good thing that happened today?

_____

_____

_____

_____

What is one lesson I learned today?

_____

_____

_____

Date:

Word of the day:

Today I am grateful for . . .

What is one good thing that happened today?

What is one lesson I learned today?

Date:

_____

Word of the day:

_____

Today I am grateful for . . .

_____
_____
_____
_____

What is one good thing that happened today?

_____
_____
_____
_____

What is one lesson I learned today?

_____
_____
_____

Date:

_____

Word of the day:

_____

Today I am grateful for . . .

_____

_____

_____

_____

What is one good thing that happened today?

_____

_____

_____

_____

What is one lesson I learned today?

_____

_____

_____

Date:

Word of the day:

Today I am grateful for . . .

What is one good thing that happened today?

What is one lesson I learned today?

Date:

_____

Word of the day:

_____

Today I am grateful for . . .

_____

_____

_____

_____

What is one good thing that happened today?

_____

_____

_____

_____

What is one lesson I learned today?

_____

_____

_____

Date:

_____

Word of the day:

_____

Today I am grateful for . . .

_____

_____

_____

_____

What is one good thing that happened today?

_____

_____

_____

_____

What is one lesson I learned today?

_____

_____

_____

_____

Date:

_____

Word of the day:

_____

Today I am grateful for . . .

_____

_____

_____

_____

What is one good thing that happened today?

_____

_____

_____

_____

What is one lesson I learned today?

_____

_____

_____

Date:

_____

Word of the day:

_____

Today I am grateful for . . .

_____

_____

_____

_____

What is one good thing that happened today?

_____

_____

_____

_____

What is one lesson I learned today?

_____

_____

_____

_____

Date:

_____

Word of the day:

_____

Today I am grateful for . . .

_____

_____

_____

_____

What is one good thing that happened today?

_____

_____

_____

_____

What is one lesson I learned today?

_____

_____

_____

_____

Date:

Word of the day:

Today I am grateful for . . .

What is one good thing that happened today?

What is one lesson I learned today?

Date:

_____

Word of the day:

_____

Today I am grateful for . . .

_____

_____

_____

_____

What is one good thing that happened today?

_____

_____

_____

_____

What is one lesson I learned today?

_____

_____

_____

_____

Date:

_____

Word of the day:

_____

Today I am grateful for . . .

_____

_____

_____

_____

What is one good thing that happened today?

_____

_____

_____

_____

What is one lesson I learned today?

_____

_____

_____

Date:

_____

Word of the day:

_____

Today I am grateful for . . .

_____

_____

_____

_____

What is one good thing that happened today?

_____

_____

_____

_____

What is one lesson I learned today?

_____

_____

_____

Date:

_____

Word of the day:

_____

Today I am grateful for . . .

_____

_____

_____

_____

What is one good thing that happened today?

_____

_____

_____

_____

What is one lesson I learned today?

_____

_____

_____

Date:

_____

Word of the day:

_____

Today I am grateful for . . .

_____

_____

_____

_____

What is one good thing that happened today?

_____

_____

_____

_____

What is one lesson I learned today?

_____

_____

_____

_____

Date:

_____

Word of the day:

_____

Today I am grateful for . . .

_____

_____

_____

_____

What is one good thing that happened today?

_____

_____

_____

_____

What is one lesson I learned today?

_____

_____

_____

Date:

_____

Word of the day:

_____

Today I am grateful for . . .

_____

_____

_____

_____

What is one good thing that happened today?

_____

_____

_____

_____

What is one lesson I learned today?

_____

_____

_____

Date:

Word of the day:

Today I am grateful for . . .

What is one good thing that happened today?

What is one lesson I learned today?

Date:

_____

Word of the day:

_____

Today I am grateful for . . .

_____
_____
_____
_____

What is one good thing that happened today?

_____
_____
_____
_____

What is one lesson I learned today?

_____
_____
_____

Date:

_____

Word of the day:

_____

Today I am grateful for . . .

_____

_____

_____

_____

What is one good thing that happened today?

_____

_____

_____

_____

What is one lesson I learned today?

_____

_____

_____

Date:

_____

Word of the day:

_____

Today I am grateful for . . .

_____

_____

_____

_____

What is one good thing that happened today?

_____

_____

_____

_____

What is one lesson I learned today?

_____

_____

_____

_____

Date:

Word of the day:

Today I am grateful for . . .

What is one good thing that happened today?

What is one lesson I learned today?

Date:

_____

Word of the day:

_____

Today I am grateful for . . .

_____

_____

_____

_____

What is one good thing that happened today?

_____

_____

_____

_____

What is one lesson I learned today?

_____

_____

_____

_____

Date:

_____

Word of the day:

_____

Today I am grateful for . . .

_____

_____

_____

_____

What is one good thing that happened today?

_____

_____

_____

_____

What is one lesson I learned today?

_____

_____

_____

Date:

_____

Word of the day:

_____

Today I am grateful for . . .

_____

_____

_____

_____

What is one good thing that happened today?

_____

_____

_____

_____

What is one lesson I learned today?

_____

_____

_____

Date:

_____

Word of the day:

_____

Today I am grateful for . . .

_____

_____

_____

_____

What is one good thing that happened today?

_____

_____

_____

_____

What is one lesson I learned today?

_____

_____

_____

Date:

_____

Word of the day:

_____

Today I am grateful for . . .

_____

_____

_____

_____

What is one good thing that happened today?

_____

_____

_____

_____

What is one lesson I learned today?

_____

_____

_____

_____

Date:

_____

Word of the day:

_____

Today I am grateful for . . .

_____

_____

_____

_____

What is one good thing that happened today?

_____

_____

_____

_____

What is one lesson I learned today?

_____

_____

_____

Date:

_____

Word of the day:

_____

Today I am grateful for . . .

_____
_____
_____
_____

What is one good thing that happened today?

_____
_____
_____
_____

What is one lesson I learned today?

_____
_____
_____

Date:

Word of the day:

Today I am grateful for . . .

What is one good thing that happened today?

What is one lesson I learned today?

Date:

_____

Word of the day:

_____

Today I am grateful for . . .

_____
_____
_____
_____

What is one good thing that happened today?

_____
_____
_____
_____

What is one lesson I learned today?

_____
_____
_____

Date:

_____

Word of the day:

_____

Today I am grateful for . . .

_____

_____

_____

_____

What is one good thing that happened today?

_____

_____

_____

_____

What is one lesson I learned today?

_____

_____

_____

Date:

_____

Word of the day:

_____

Today I am grateful for . . .

_____

_____

_____

_____

What is one good thing that happened today?

_____

_____

_____

_____

What is one lesson I learned today?

_____

_____

_____

Date:

_____

Word of the day:

_____

Today I am grateful for . . .

_____

_____

_____

_____

What is one good thing that happened today?

_____

_____

_____

_____

What is one lesson I learned today?

_____

_____

_____

Date:

_____

Word of the day:

_____

Today I am grateful for . . .

_____

_____

_____

_____

What is one good thing that happened today?

_____

_____

_____

_____

What is one lesson I learned today?

_____

_____

_____

Date:

Word of the day:

Today I am grateful for . . .

What is one good thing that happened today?

What is one lesson I learned today?

Date:

_____

Word of the day:

_____

Today I am grateful for . . .

_____

_____

_____

_____

What is one good thing that happened today?

_____

_____

_____

_____

What is one lesson I learned today?

_____

_____

_____

Date:

_____

Word of the day:

_____

Today I am grateful for . . .

_____

_____

_____

_____

What is one good thing that happened today?

_____

_____

_____

_____

What is one lesson I learned today?

_____

_____

_____

Date:

_____

Word of the day:

_____

Today I am grateful for . . .

_____
_____
_____
_____

What is one good thing that happened today?

_____
_____
_____
_____

What is one lesson I learned today?

_____
_____
_____

freestyle

Use these pages to write about anything and everything!

about the author

MISTY COPELAND made history by becoming the first female African American principal dancer at the American Ballet Theatre. The bestselling author of *Life in Motion* and a children's picture book, *Firebird*, she has been the recipient of the Leonore Annenberg Fellowship in the Arts and an inductee into the Boys & Girls Clubs of America Alumni Hall of Fame. In 2015 Misty was named to the TIME 100 and was one of *Glamour* magazine's Women of the Year. She lives in New York City. Visit her at mistycopeland.com.